Strategy and Tactics
How the left can organise to transform society

John Rees

a COUNTERFIRE publication

Strategy and Tactics
How the left can organise to transform society

First published in Great Britain in 2010 by Counterfire, 137 Maryland
Road, London N22 5AS

ISBN 978-1-907899-00-3

A catalogue record for this book is available from the British Library

Printed and bound in Great Britain

Contents

Introduction: What is to be done?   5

1. What are we aiming for?   7

2. Whose strategy, whose tactics?   11

3. Revolutionary organisation   15

4. Sectarianism and liquidationism   19

5. Political organisation and class struggle   23

6. Timing in revolutionary politics   27

7. Seizing the key link   31

8. What are cadre?   35

9. Propaganda and agitation   39

10. The united front   43

11. Ultra-leftism   49

12. Marxism and the trade unions   53

13. The Marxist method   59

Further reading   65

Introduction:
What is to be done?

'What is to be done?' is the essential question at the heart of Marxism. Strategic and tactical decisions are about just this question. How do we organise to act? What methods, what arguments, will best enable us to change the society around us in the ways we wish?

Many people will say that there is so much more to Marxism than strategy and tactics. Marxism is a theory of history, a philosophy, an economic theory, a political theory, and so on. And of course this is true. But in Marxism the whole point of this vast panoply of analysis is to bring us to the point where we have the knowledge to act effectively. As Marx's famous 11th thesis on Feuerbach has it, 'The philosophers have only *interpreted* the world, in various ways, the point is to *change* it.'

So Marxism is distinguished from all other sociological theories and left-wing doctrines by its insistence on answering the 'What is to be done?' question. Other doctrines, academic and political, may analyse and observe the social reality around them, but it is Marxism's commitment to acting upon such analyses that marks it out.

This commitment to the unity of theory and practice points toward some other fundamental aspects of Marxism. It raises the question, for instance, of who is going to do whatever it is that needs to be done. That is, it asks this question: which class and what political actors in that class are capable of making change happen?

In asking this question, the question of agency, it must therefore ask a further question: from what point of view should we analyse and observe historical development?

This question runs right to the heart of the debate between academic sociology and Marxism, because it requires us to consider whether the truth about the society we live in will be better revealed from the standpoint of its central exploited class, the working class, or from a detached, 'neutral' point of view.

Strategic and tactical decisions are, then, at the heart of Marxism, and they rest on a much broader and deeper analysis of the class structure of capitalist society and on ways of viewing the world that arise from that society.

The early sections of this pamphlet take a brief look at these issues in order to provide a framework for the discussion of strategy and tactics. But the later sections always refer back to this framework, and it is always the presupposition on which later discussion rests. There is always the closest connection between general theory and strategy and tactics in Marxism, even if the connections are not necessarily obvious.

When, in 1902, Lenin took the title *What is to be done?* for what became one of his most famous pamphlets, he did so at a time when the forces of the revolutionaries in Russia were scattered and weak. But his persistence in answering this question, at that time and afterwards, brought them to the point where they could play a decisive role in the Russian Revolution. If revolutionaries are to play a constructive role in the battles that working people face today, they must still have the strategic and tactical capacity to answer that same question.

1. What are we aiming for?

The phrase 'strategy and tactics' is military in origin. Armies have strategic war aims and they adapt their tactics to overcome the problems they face in battle in ways that move them towards their strategic goal.

The great Russian revolutionary Leon Trotsky wrote: 'By tactics in politics, we understand, using the analogy of military science, the art of conducting isolated operations. By strategy, we understand the art of conquest, i.e. the seizure of power.'

Indeed, Trotsky's very distinction between tactics and strategy, which Lenin shared, was borrowed from the German military theorist von Clausewitz. One of the reasons this definition became important to Lenin and Trotsky was that it allowed them to insist that tactics are subordinate to strategic goals.

Before the crisis in the Second International caused by the First World War, in which most of the socialist movement's leaders abandoned internationalism and sided with their own ruling classes in supporting the carnage in the trenches, this way of looking at strategy and tactics was not common.

'Before the war we did not, as a rule, make this distinction,' writes Trotsky. 'In the epoch of the Second International we confined ourselves solely to the conception of social democratic tactics. Nor was this accidental.'

It was not accidental, in Trotsky's view, because the Second International had in reality abandoned the goal of socialist revolution. All that was left for it was a series of tactical activities unrelated to the goal of revolution – aiming, in fact, at simply reforming the existing system.

Thus, the social-democratic parties had trade union

tactics, parliamentary tactics, municipal tactics, and so on, but 'the question of combining all forces and resources – all sorts of troops – to obtain victory over the enemy was never really raised in the epoch of the Second International, insofar as the task of the struggle for power was not raised.'

This question was re-imposed on the movement first by the 1905 Revolution in Russia, and then again by the outbreak of war in 1914 and the Russian Revolution of 1917. After that, the worldwide revolutionary turmoil of the post-war years persistently raised the issue of political power for the working class everywhere from Germany in 1918 to China in 1926 through to Spain in 1936.

That is why this era is so fruitful for a study of strategy and tactics – but similar questions are raised in every serious class struggle and every revolution.

In these circumstances, military analogies like strategy and tactics will always be valuable, because political analysis and warfare have something crucial in common. They are both great simplifiers: they demand a focus on the essential and a ruthless relegation of the inessential.

One of the most difficult tasks in deciding strategy and tactics is to draw out of the mass of information and events that swirl around us what our key goals should be and what basic methods we should adopt to achieve them. This, inevitably, means treating as secondary many facets of the situation that to others may seem vital.

This same business of prioritisation is of course central in warfare. One cannot, either strategically or tactically, afford to waste resources on those fronts that are not essential. One has to 'abstract' from the chaos of war those fronts that are essential and concentrate forces at them.

But this process of abstraction – the selection of critical areas of activity – then has to be tested in practice. Is it true that if we concentrate forces at this point we can make a breakthrough? After making an assessment, there is only one way to find out – try it and see!

Lenin liked to quote Napoleon's advice: 'Let's engage in battle and then we'll see.' At a certain point, all theoretical, strategic, and tactical disputes can be resolved only in practice.

Or as Trotsky put it when condemning the 'barren scholasticism' of endless debate:

> It would be analogous to wrangling over the advantages of various systems of swimming while we stubbornly refused to turn our eyes to the river where swimmers were putting these systems into practice. No better test of the viewpoints concerning revolution exist than the verification of how they worked out during the revolution itself, just as a system of swimming is best tested when a swimmer jumps into the water.

2. Whose strategy, whose tactics?

Every organisation has strategy and tactics. Armies obviously have strategies and tactics. So do corporations, NGOs, charities, trade unions, governments, and political parties. But the strategy and tactics you adopt depend on the kind of organisation you are in. Moreover, differences in strategy arise because of the differing class base of the various organisations in society.

So although it seems obvious that discussion of strategy and tactics should be about the most immediate and pressing campaigns in which we are involved, in fact, such discussion must start much further back. It must begin much deeper in the social structure.

We, of course, are interested in the working class and its capacity for resisting the system. So let us look at some of the key characteristics of workers in capitalist society.

Workers are an exploited and oppressed class. They have to work for a wage which represents only part of the wealth that their work produces – the rest creates profits for the owners of the factories, offices, mines, transport systems, information technologies, power industries, supermarkets, and all the other accumulated economic wealth of society.

This subordination has its counterpart in the ideas that workers hold, at least some of the time. Economic and political subordination breeds passivity and fatalism. Some of the clichés we learn early in life express this: 'the poor are always with us', 'there will always be the rich man in his castle and the poor man at his gate', 'so it's been, so it will always be'.

It is not surprising that many workers accept these ideas,

at least partially. Their economic subordination involves being told when to work and when not, how hard to work and at what, what they will be paid, and how much they will have to pay for what they produce when it reappears on the market.

This lack of control over the productive core of society – what Karl Marx called 'alienation' – does not encourage ideological independence.

Every conservative, from the heads of corporations to the leaders of the Tory Party, relies on the passivity induced by powerlessness. It provides soil within which acceptance of the *status quo* takes root.

So is our situation hopeless? Are we in an Orwellian 1984-like nightmare where a completely divided and atomised working class is constantly disoriented and immobilised by the propaganda of our rulers? Is this not the Tory dream of a working class without the capacity for revolt? If this were true, our discussion of strategy and tactics would be a short one. No strategy is possible where no resistance takes place.

But alienation is only half the picture. The system always induces revolt as well as passivity. The exploitation and oppression that working people and other groups suffer have always provoked resistance, revolt, and revolution. There always comes a point where some group of workers somewhere decide that enough is enough and that they must take some kind of action.

But if the Tory dream of absolute passivity among working people is untrue, we must not think that its opposite, the anarchist dream of perpetual and spontaneous revolt among workers, is true either.

In reality, there is always a battle between where workers interests lie – in combating the system – and where their consciousness is at any given time – which involves acceptance of the system at least to some degree.

Some critics of Marxism say that this distinction – between workers' interests and their consciousness – is an artificial one invented to explain away that fact that workers ought to oppose the system but often go along with it. How can you say, the critics ask, that workers have interests different from the views they express?

But this is really not a difficult idea to defend. In everyday life, we all accept that individuals' interests can be different from their consciousness. Look at people who smoke cigarettes. We, and they, know where their interests lie. They lie in giving up smoking, because, as it says in large letters on every packet of cigarettes, 'Smoking Kills'. Yet their consciousness does not register this fact and they go on smoking.

We think we have some insight into why people behave like this: peer group pressure, advertising, family example, stress, and so on. And many of the same social pressures, on a much greater scale, exist to persuade people not to strike, join a union, riot, or make revolution.

The result is that most workers, most of the time, have what the Italian Marxist Antonio Gramsci called 'contradictory consciousness'. They accept certain things about the system while rejecting others. They may be anti-racists, but admire the Queen. Or they may be great trade-union militants, but believe in immigration controls. The variety of such contradictions is endless.

The aim of socialists must be to raise the level of consciousness and combativity among workers. They must find a way to act with workers in such a way that the more conservative elements of this contradictory consciousness are reduced and the more progressive strengthened.

This is what socialist strategy and tactics are all about: finding those organisations, slogans, and ideas that counteract conservatism and passivity among workers and instead encourage them to fight back.

3. Revolutionary organisation

Leon Trotsky once said that five workers that he met early in his political life told him everything he needed to know about the need for socialist organisation.

The gist of Trotsky's story is this: one of the five workers was a dyed-in-the-wool reactionary – he would never join a union, he was a racist and a sexist, and, if there were a strike, he would scab. Another of the five was the exact opposite – a good union activist, an anti-racist, and a socialist always willing to stand up for the underdog.

Between these two polar opposites were the other three workers. They could sometimes be swayed by the arguments of the reactionary, leaving the socialist isolated. But they could also be won to the arguments of the socialist, leaving the reactionary isolated.

Trotsky's point was this: a revolutionary organisation must seek out and relate to the minority of socialists, because by becoming part of a network that produces a paper, holds meetings, develops explanations of the world, and organises action, the minority, the one in five, will become clearer and tougher about their politics, and better able to win over their fellow workers.

This short fable crystallises two critical Marxist views of working class struggle. It highlights the uneven consciousness of the working class (discussed in the last chapter) and it proposes that a minority or 'vanguard' organisation is the most effective tool for overcoming this unevenness in a progressive way.

The most advanced sections of the international working class movement after the Russian Revolution of 1917 reached the same conclusion. Generalising from the success of Lenin's Bolsheviks, they concluded that only 'a party of a new type' (in the phrase used by the newly founded Communist International) could be effective in leading workers' struggles.

The Hungarian revolutionary Georg Lukacs expressed this idea in its simplest and most direct form: 'the militant minority must assemble in the form of an organisation.'

This may seem like an elementary point, but, in fact, the exact opposite of this form of organisation was almost universal in the working class movement before 1917 and remains the most common form of workers' organisation today.

The Labour Party model of organisation is deliberately *not* a vanguard organisation. It is a broad party that seeks to encompass most, if not all, working class opinion. In the terms of Trotsky's metaphor, it seeks to unite at least four of the five workers in the same organisation. Unlike a vanguard organisation, it seeks to unite them in the same party whether or not they agree with the militant.

Such parties were the accepted norm in the Second International that dominated the labour movement internationally between the 1880s and 1917. They have remained the model for electoralist Labour and social-democratic parties internationally ever since.

The strength of such parties is obvious: they are big. But their weakness is fatal and it undermines this strength: they are divided politically between a radical minority and a conservative or, at best, confused and vacillating majority. This is absolutely inevitable in a working class that has uneven consciousness. A broad party is bound to reproduce this unevenness.

The effect of alienation, the separation between the interests and the consciousness of the working class, the effects of the media, the education system, and so on, all mean that a majority of workers, most of the time, will not share the overall or general views of the radical socialist minority.

Add this to the conservative bureaucracy of MPs, councillors, trade union leaders, and other functionaries that dominate the upper reaches of electoralist parties and we can easily see why such organisations almost always abandon their principles at decisive or difficult turning points in the class struggle.

This is exactly what happened to the parties of the Second International at the outset of the First World War. For decades, they declared opposition to war and threatened a united general strike of workers to prevent war should it look imminent. On the day, virtually all the national parties and in particular the greatest of them, the German Social Democratic Party, collapsed into jingoistic support for their own rulers.

In Britain, we have before our eyes over a century of Labour Party history to demonstrate the failure of this type of organisation to take us one step nearer to socialism. Indeed, we can show that on most occasions the conservative majority in the party manages to silence or reduce to ineffectiveness the radical minority.

It was just such experience that drove revolutionary socialists to the conclusion that there must be a different organisational relationship between the militant minority and the rest of the class. Rather than being together in one organisation where the minority was subordinated to conservative forces, the minority had to form its own radical organisation able to organise and operate freely.

But this immediately raises the issue of how this vanguard should relate to, aim to organise, and strive to win over the rest of the working class. How does the minority prevent itself becoming a self-satisfied sect that is never able to lead effective action by the majority of workers?

This, indeed, is a fundamental problem of revolution. For if a revolution is the democratic act of the majority of the working class, if the revolution is, in Marx's phrase, the 'self-emancipation of the working class', how does an organisation of the militant minority relate to this wider movement?

This is the core question of revolutionary strategy and tactics.

4. Sectarianism and liquidationism

An organised grouping of revolutionary socialists, independent of all influence except that of working class struggle, is the indispensable prerequisite for any revolutionary strategy.

Without such organisational independence, revolutionaries will find themselves tied to the more conservative layers of the working class and, therefore, to the influence of the ruling class and its ideologues among the middle classes and the labour movement bureaucracy.

But once such an independent revolutionary organisation, resting on the most advanced sections of the class, exists it must immediately find a way of relating to the wider struggles of the working class.

In the years after the Russian Revolution, Lenin urged revolutionaries in Italy to break with Turati, the leader of the reformist Italian Socialist Party (SP), and create their own independent revolutionary Communist Party (CP).

Nevertheless, Lenin also realised that many very good workers would remain in Turati's party and would not immediately join the CP. He insisted that the Italian revolutionaries should continue to work with, relate to, and address these SP supporters, even though they refused to join the CP.

Lenin's advise to the Italian revolutionaries was: 'you must break with Turati in order to unite with Turati'. He did not say this because he had any faith in Turati – rather the opposite: he wanted Italian revolutionaries to work alongside SP supporters in order to undermine *their* faith in Turati.

This example highlights the twin dangers that face any independent revolutionary organisation: liquidationism and sectarianism. Not to break from the SP would have been to 'liquidate' (dissolve) the revolutionaries into a social-democratic or reformist party and neuter them as an independent force.

Of course, they might still have been able to make revolutionary speeches and propose motions that embodied their own ideas within the SP. They might have hoped, over the long term, in this way, to win the majority of the Socialist Party to their views. This was the course that Rosa Luxemburg adopted in the German Social Democratic Party before 1914.

But what she lacked then – and what the Italian revolutionaries would have lacked if they had not left the SP and formed an independent organisation as Lenin advised – was any capacity for independent *action*. She was – as they would have been – a prisoner inside a social-democratic party. The danger in this situation is that the activity of revolutionaries is shaped by the rhythm and direction of electoralist and reformist politics, not by the requirements of the class struggle.

But if Lenin had not also insisted that, as soon as they had created an independent organisation, the Italian revolutionaries then seek every opportunity for joint action and common struggle with SP supporters, they would have been guilty of the equal and opposite error of sectarianism. This means attempting to insulate yourself from conservative influence and create a 'pure' socialist organisation in isolation from the majority of the working class.

Marx was forthright against this as far back as 1848, writing in *The Communist Manifesto*:

> *The Communists do not form a separate party opposed to other working-class parties. They have no interests separate and apart from those of the*

*proletariat as a whole. They do not set up any
sectarian principles of their own, by which to shape
and mould the proletarian movement.*

Lenin's idea of a revolutionary party seems to contradict
this. But this is only really true if the non-sectarian
purpose of Marx's injunction is ignored. It would be
sectarian, for instance, for revolutionaries to refuse to join
trade unions on the grounds that they are not socialist
organisations and do not fight to overthrow capitalism,
but merely for better pay and conditions. Workers need
unity on the most basic economic issues. Socialists should
therefore be the best trade unionists, not people who stand
on the sidelines preaching about the need for an alternative
to capitalism.

Since it is often precisely through the experience of
such struggles that workers become aware of the limits of
trade unionism and of the need for socialism, it is not only
sectarian but also counter-productive for revolutionaries
not to be central to the fight.

In recent years, in Britain, we have often seen small
groups on the left stand aside from, or take a sectarian
attitude towards, the anti-war movement, because it is
not, in their view, sufficiently 'anti-imperialist'. What they
mean is that not everyone involved is opposed in principle
to imperialism as a global system. This is true, but if
revolutionaries do not throw themselves into the anti-war
movement, how will they ever persuade anti-war activists
that the best way to oppose war is to be consistently anti-
imperialist?

Tony Cliff, the author of a path-breaking biography
of Lenin, used to underline the dangers of sectarianism
and liquidationism with this example. Imagine you are on
a picket line, he used to say, and the striker next to you
makes a racist remark. There are three things you can do
in response.

The first is to ignore the racist comment and talk about

the weather. This is unprincipled and liquidationist – you have just collapsed your own anti-racist politics and ignored a remark you should have challenged. The second is to protest at the racist remark and walk self-righteously off the picket line. This is sectarian, because although you have demonstrated your principles, you have weakened the strike and may help strike-breakers defeat it.

The right thing to do is to argue with the person making the racist remark, but stay on the picket line – and if the strike-breakers arrive, you should link arms with the person you are arguing with so that together you can stop them getting through. This creates the essential bond of solidarity which gives you a chance of winning the political argument.

This example underlines the point that both sectarianism and liquidationism have the same root: impatience with the speed of development of the consciousness of the working class. The liquidationist wants to short-cut the long struggle to raise the combativity and consciousness of the working class by dissolving into it in its current state. The sectarians want to ignore the current state of the working class by cutting themselves off and subsisting in a cocoon of revolutionary purity.

Both forms of impatience have the same result: nothing changes.

5. Political organisation and class struggle

If a revolutionary organisation is the most advanced part of the working class, how does it relate to the rest of the working class and to the wider struggles of the working class? The first step in understanding this relationship is to grasp that although a revolutionary network of militants seeks to organise the most advanced sections of the class, it cannot substitute for the working class as a whole.

The party does not and cannot make a revolution. This must be the act of the majority of the working class, not just its most advanced section. At the very moment of the October Revolution in 1917, the leaders of the Bolshevik Party military organisation argued that it should be this party body that organised the seizure of power. Lenin opposed them. He insisted that it could not be a party organisation that made the revolution. He was absolutely clear that it must be the military organisation of the Workers' Council that should accomplish the task.

The party represented only part of the working class, whereas the Workers' Council included representatives from the broadest swathes of the class. Lenin's reasoning was clear: the Bolsheviks may have been able to provide political leadership at decisive moments but it is only when this lead was taken up and acted on by a majority of the working class that such action was effective. In the old phrase, 'Man proposes, God disposes'; in revolutionary politics, the party may propose, but the working class disposes.

In any case, any organisation's ideas, and its role as a vanguard, can only be sustained if it learns from working class struggle.

The claim to be a vanguard rests on the revolutionary minority's ability to condense and express the best experiences of working class struggle. This is not achieved in a single moment at the time of the organisation's formation and assumed to remain the case ever after. It must be constantly renewed.

Frederick Engels made the point that all really innovative military tactics were discovered by rank-and-file soldiers under the impact of emergency conditions in the heat of warfare. The job of a good military leadership was to recognise such advances, even if they conflicted with established theory and practice, and to generalise them throughout the army.

Lukacs makes the same point: 'in no sense is the party's role to impose any kind of abstract, cleverly devised tactics on the masses. On the contrary, it must continuously *learn* from their struggle and…unite the spontaneous discoveries…with the totality of the revolutionary struggle, and bring them to consciousness.'

Lukacs is here pointing to a double process: the revolutionary minority must learn from the class, but it must also unite what it learns with 'the totality of the revolutionary struggle'. But what is this totality, and how is it to be united with what is learnt from the class?

The totality of the struggle is the accumulated historical experience of the working class in its battle with capitalism. This means not just the historical experience in an immediate sense – what happened in the 1984-85 miners' strike, or the poll tax campaign, or in 1968, or in the General Strike of 1926, and so on. It also means the more theorised experience of how capitalism works economically, how imperialism works, how to judge various philosophies, religions, or art forms.

Only a political organisation is capable of organising such an educational experience on a broad scale for thousands (or perhaps tens of thousands) of militants in the working class movement. This is the meaning of the idea that the revolutionary organisation is both 'the memory of the class' and 'the university of the class'.

And how do we know if we have learnt the right lessons or made the correct theoretical generalisations? Only the practice of the organisation and the class will tell. As Marx expressed it: 'the question of whether objective truth can be attributed to human thinking is not a question of theory but is a *practical* question. Man must prove the truth, i.e. the reality and power, the this-sidedness of his thinking in practice.'

The revolutionary organisation can perform its role only through an interactive, dialectical relationship with working class struggle. The party both learns from and summarises the past experience of the struggle. It proposes action based on what it has learnt. And it assesses the correctness of these proposals according to what it learns anew from its conscious attempt to intervene in the struggles of workers.

6. Timing in revolutionary politics

The activity of a revolutionary organisation forms part of a chain of events taking place over time. The revolutionary minority never controls the whole chain, because it is composed of economic factors, the actions of other political organisations, the consciousness and combativity of the working class, and many other elements that are either wholly or partially independent of the influence of the organised minority.

A network of revolutionaries *can* have a crucial effect on the course of events, but *only* if it accurately gauges the way in which these other factors are shaping them, and if it tailors its actions to promote some outcomes and suppress others. Moreover, and crucially, since the weight of these factors and the overall direction of events are constantly changing, what a revolutionary organisation may be able to achieve at one time may not be achievable even a short time later.

In short, the question of timing is crucial. This is never more true than in the timing of revolution itself.

Here is one less well-known example from the English Revolution. In 1647, after the First Civil War, King Charles was being feted by the moderates in the House of Commons. If they had been successful, the radicals in the New Model Army, the decisive revolutionary force at this moment, would have been marginalised, and the revolution might never have achieved its full stature.

But decisive action by Cromwell – who vacillated before and after attempting to come to a treaty with the King – and the Army radicals, led to the seizure of Charles by a troop of horses commanded by Cornet Joyce (a very junior officer). Asked by the King for his commission for the arrest, Joyce simply pointed to the troopers behind him. Had the King not been taken prisoner by the Army, he might have been restored to the throne.

A more famous example comes from the Russian Revolution. The period immediately before the October insurrection was one of confusion among the leaders of the Bolshevik Party. Lenin wrote letter after letter urging preparations for a new insurrection. Lenin's tone is frantic in this correspondence because he believed that delay would be disastrous: 'Delay is criminal. To wait…would be…a betrayal of the revolution.' And again: 'to miss such a moment…would be *utter idiocy*, or *sheer treachery*…for it would mean losing weeks at a time when weeks and even days decide *everything*. It would mean faint-heartedly *renouncing* power, for on 1-2 November it will have become impossible to take power.'

Finally, after he had threatened resignation from the Central Committee, the Party's leading body, Lenin's view prevailed and the insurrection took place on 25 October 1917.

It is not always the case that urgency means a matter of days. In a revolution, as Lenin noted elsewhere, developments that normally take years can be contracted into days, even hours.

But there is, nevertheless, always a window of opportunity outside which certain actions will no longer be possible or will not have the same force. In recent history, for instance, had revolutionaries not decided to launch the Stop the War Coalition within days of the attack on the Twin Towers, it is unlikely that it would have had the same galvanising effect that it did.

Of course, it is also possible to move too quickly. Had the Bolsheviks attempted a revolution in the summer of 1917, when reaction was in the air, it would certainly have rebounded on them, strengthening the counter-revolution, perhaps decisively. At this time, the Bolsheviks worked to restrain those who wanted to push forward and launch an insurrection. But whether one is urging restraint or advance, issuing a clear call at the appropriate time is essential.

Many years ago, the labour historian Ralph Samuel wrote that one of the things he disliked about the Communist Party was that there was always a tone of emergency in the organisation. Something or other always had to be 'done now', 'could not wait', and so on. This criticism is misplaced. If a revolutionary organisation is to play its role in the chain of events, whatever that role might be at any given time, it must act with dispatch. There is always something to be done, and, if it is to be done to maximum effect, it needs to be done in a timely manner.

But 'timely' is a variable quantity. What is necessary to prepare for imminent revolution may have to be accomplished with greater speed than the preparation for a demonstration in normal times that is six months hence. But since all organisations, even revolutionary organisations, produce their own inertia, adhering to past patterns of work even when new challenges arise, there will always be a battle to turn the organisation to a correct orientation in good time.

Other political forces, both enemies and rivals, will not wait. So timing will always be of the essence for revolutionaries. Duncan Hallas, a leading revolutionary socialist and the author of a very useful study of Trotsky, used to quote Shakespeare to make the point:

There is a tide in the affairs of men,
Which, taken at the flood, leads on to fortune;
Omitted, all the voyage of their life,
Is bound in shallows and in miseries.
On such a full sea are we now afloat,
And we must take the current when it serves,
Or lose our ventures.

7. Seizing the key link

In all Lenin's writing on strategy and tactics, there are few more important passages than this one:

> Every question "runs in a vicious circle" because political life as a whole is an endless chain consisting of an infinite number of links. The whole art of politics lies in finding and taking as firm a grip as we can of the link that is least likely to be struck from our hands, the one most important at the given moment, the one that most guarantees its possessor the possession of the whole chain.

This is a profound insight for a number of reasons. It very accurately describes how many people first experience political reality. A whole host of issues, all equally important from a general point of view, assail them from every direction. Global warming, racism, trade union struggle, war, abortion, civil liberties – these and many more are all important, all demand our attention. Each one will have its specialist advocates, and they will often have a good case.

A frequent response to this dilemma is to try and do everything. But this rarely leads to effective political work, even for individuals, never mind entire organisations. Another response, for organisations, is to allow their members to pick and chose what work they do according to their own preferences. This is common in reformist, Labour Party-type organisations. Since all they really care about is electoral activity, this is the only time they require an organisation-wide focus from every member. For the rest of the time, members can be active in whatever campaign most takes their fancy.

But this 'buffet lunch' approach (come when you like, eat as much or as little as you like, of whatever you like) can develop in any organisation that is not ruthlessly focused on the key issues. And the approach is fundamentally wrong because the world is not in fact a chaos of competing issues all of more or less equal weight.

It is actually a series of related issues, all of which trace their origin back to the essential class contradictions of capitalist society. Global warming, war, racism, and so on are all in their different and specific forms consequences of the anarchic pursuit of profit that governs the system and of the class and other struggles that it generates. At any given time, the struggle that is most likely to challenge the system can arise in any one of these areas. The knack of understanding which is the 'key link' is therefore a question of theoretical analysis.

Here is a contemporary example: it is obvious now that imperialism is a key link in current global politics. But to see this during the First Gulf War, or the Balkan War, or even in the immediate aftermath of 9/11 required a preceding analysis of the 'new imperialism' that arose after the Cold War.

As Lenin points out: 'anybody who tackles the partial problems without having previously settled general problems, will inevitably and at every step "come up against" those general problems without realising it. To come up against them blindly and in every individual case means to doom one's politics to the worst vacillation and lack of principle.'

Without an analysis of the new imperialism, it would not have been possible to see the anti-war movement emerging as a key link and to make this central to the work of revolutionaries. Moreover, to get the necessary focus on this key link, it was essential to mount a specific campaign on the left more widely over a period of weeks and months.

This 'bending the stick', as Lenin called it, is a ruthless form of prioritisation in which other, often in themselves important issues are relegated to second place. This inevitably requires internal discussion and argument inside an organisation. Old priorities, quite correct in their time, have to be superseded. Understandable but often moralistic objections to 'neglecting' other areas of work have to be addressed.

Come what may, there is no avoiding the requirement to define and grasp the key link. Look how the recession in all its aspects (the general election, the coalition government, the financial crisis, the budget cuts, the attacks on jobs, wages, pensions, and services, etc.) surged to the top of the political agenda in Spring 2010. Any socialist organisation that does not shape a wide-ranging response to this crisis and pursue it ruthlessly would simply prove itself not fit for purpose.

Does this mean that all other areas of political work are ignored? No. But at all times, the party must prioritise. Lenin's point is that grasping the key link 'guarantees its possessor the possession of the whole chain'. Forces accumulated on the key front can then be deployed in other areas of struggle according to their importance. Successes on one critical issue will lift the confidence of those struggling on other fronts.

We know from recent history how successes in the anti-globalisation struggles that followed the great Seattle demonstration in 1999 underpinned the launch of the anti-war movement. If revolutionaries had not focused on the anti-capitalist struggles, even though they were smaller in this country than elsewhere, they would not have been as well placed to launch and sustain the anti-war movement – even though the anti-war movement then required their full attention, 'to the detriment' of earlier anti-globalisation work.

The final point is simple but vital: the best form of continuity between all these different fronts and different phases of the struggle is the revolutionary network. At each turn, it must seek to recruit and sustain a group of activists who see the whole of the class struggle in all its different forms as their political home, and who are able to focus their whole attention on each vital question as it arises in the course of that struggle.

8. What are cadre?

Anyone who is active in left-wing politics for very long will soon come across the term 'cadre'. It has come to mean a group of activists who have a certain level of political understanding and practical organising experience.

It is easy to see why any organisation would want to develop such a body of members. It gives the organisation weight and effectiveness in the struggle. It enables it to integrate new members into a political tradition. And it should give the organisation the ability to operate effectively in a wide range of different struggles and different phases of struggle.

Such members are also often, though not always, more rooted in the trade unions and working class organisations. They have more 'weight' in the movement and so can be more effective in moving sections of the class in a particular direction than those who are less so.

Tactical flexibility is only possible for an organisation that has a high degree of unanimity about its basic principles, and this requires a stable group of members who understand and transmit these ideas to other comrades and across the generations.

The cadre of the organisation gives it stability, durability, and effectiveness in the struggle. But this can also give rise to problems, especially when the conditions of struggle change quickly. Trotsky explained the problem like this:

> *Each party, even the most revolutionary party, must inevitably produce its own organisational conservatism; for otherwise it would lack the necessary stability. This is wholly a question of degree. In a revolutionary party, the vitally necessary dose of conservatism must be combined with a complete freedom from routine, with initiative in orientation*

and daring in action.

This highlights an important point: cadre only remain cadre if they continue to relate correctly to the turning points in the struggle. If they do not, in spite of their accumulated knowledge and experience, they turn from an asset into a liability. Here is Trotsky again:

> *Even the most revolutionary parties, when an abrupt change occurs in the situation and a new task arises as a consequence, frequently pursue the political line of yesterday and thereby become, or threaten to become, a brake on the revolutionary process. Both conservatism and revolutionary initiative find their most concentrated expression in the leading organs of the party.*

Especially at such times, new members of the organisation may much more accurately understand what is necessary for the party to act effectively. In such circumstances, the old cliché about revolutionary parties being about 'top-down leadership' is further from the truth than ever.

In the period before the October insurrection, when the leadership of the Bolsheviks were united against Lenin's call for a second revolution (already discussed in the previous chapter, 'Timing in revolutionary politics'), it was the most advanced section of the class and the most dynamic elements in the Bolshevik Party that overcame this conservatism.

It is in this way that the cadre of the party renews itself. In such moments, it retains those who have moved with the times and integrates and educates those new cadre who have proved capable of leading in new circumstances. In this way, the debates and actions of the party constantly test the old cadre and create new leaders.

Lenin had faced this problem before 1917. As the

Bolshevik Party began to form, following a split with the more moderate Mensheviks, he had insisted that the creation of tightly-organised committees of trusted party members in as many town and cities as possible was the key.

These 'committee-men' were, Lenin's wife Krupskaya recalled, 'self assured…and did not like innovations. They were neither desirous nor capable of adapting themselves to changing conditions.'

When the 1905 Revolution broke out, these committee-men on whom Lenin had relied refused to open up the party and its structures to newly radicalised workers.

Now Lenin reversed his previous emphasis: 'Really, I sometimes think that nine-tenths of the Bolsheviks are actually formalists… We need young forces.'

The lesson is this: cadre are not defined simply as those who know Marxist theory and have much experience of the struggle. They are certainly not defined simply by age or by the length of time they have been in the party.

These advantages only remain advantages if the cadre are capable of bringing them to bear on the struggles of the day, using their experience to understand, explain, and act *in new circumstances*. For this to happen, they must be active party members who are attempting to shape the struggle by conscious intervention, not simply observing and commenting on it from afar.

In *What is to be done?*, Lenin draws a contrast between the economic leadership given to the working class movement by a trade union secretary and the kind of leadership he thinks a revolutionary socialist should give:

> *The secretary of any, say English, trade union, always helps the workers to carry on the economic struggle. He helps them to expose factory abuses, explains the injustice of the laws and the measures to hamper the freedom to strike and to picket… explains the partiality of arbitration court judges*

who belong to the bourgeois classes, etc, etc... It cannot be too strongly maintained that this is still not Social Democracy [i.e. revolutionary socialism]. The Social Democrat's ideal should not be the trade union secretary, but the tribune of the people, who is able to react to every manifestation of tyranny and oppression, no matter what stratum or class of the people it affects; who is able to generalise all these manifestations and produce a single picture of police violence and capitalist exploitation; who is able to take advantage of every event, however small, in order to set forth before all his socialist convictions...

9. Propaganda and agitation

Every active socialist has to carry out two broad tasks in the class struggle. One is to educate and the other is to organise. Education is about bringing the accumulated historical and theoretical experience of working class struggle to bear on contemporary politics. How can we analyse the recession or modern imperialism if we do not have a grasp of Marxist economics or the theory of imperialism?

But this understanding cannot simply be the private intellectual accomplishment of those already in a revolutionary organisation. It should and must be spread as widely as possible in the wider working class movement.

The word 'propaganda' has a largely pejorative flavour in everyday speech. It is associated with party-hack formulations of the Nazi or Stalinist regimes. But there is a more positive meaning that simply implies a series of relatively complex ideas like those contained in Marxist theory that one is attempting to disseminate.

When today we talk about how the recession shows that the market is automatically prone to periodic crisis, that the capitalist system is exploitative, and that it underlines the need for a new society based on collective ownership of the economy, we are propagandising. What we are not doing is suggesting that we can take immediate action on the basis of these ideas. We cannot, in other words, immediately set about abolishing the market and building socialism.

This does not diminish the vitally important task of spreading these ideas in the working class movement. But if we are talking about what we can do now, say, about the recession, then we need other, simpler, more direct ideas. These are agitational slogans.

They concern immediate action. 'Strike now against below-inflation pay offers' is an agitational slogan, especially in those unions where a ballot over taking action against a low pay offer is taking place. 'March to get the troops out now' is a direct call to action for the anti-war movement. Both these things can and should happen now. Whether or not they do depends on a subjective argument in the movement. They may or may not happen, but, unlike abolishing the market, the political forces exist in the here-and-now that could make them happen if socialists and others win the argument with those around them.

There is another form of demand that lies between the two extremes of propaganda and agitation: concrete propaganda. By this we mean a demand which a majority of workers think is possible and desirable, but which, alone, they do not have the power to enact. They think that someone else – the government or the trade union leaders – should make it happen.

The demand for a windfall tax on corporate profits is a good example. The movement can mobilise around these demands in the first instance, and, if momentum builds, they may become directly agitational in their own right. For instance, if a movement develops demanding that pensioners be given free heating, and the government refuses, the pensioners may then begin a non-payment campaign. This, of course, is what happened under Margaret Thatcher when the demand to *abolish* the poll tax developed into a *non-payment* campaign.

The Russian Marxist George Plekhanov, from whom Lenin learnt much in his early years, gives us a useful definition that can help us think clearly about this issue.

'A sect,' wrote Plekhanov, 'can be satisfied with propaganda in the narrow sense of the word: a political party never… A propagandist gives many ideas to one or a few people, while an agitator gives one or only a few ideas to masses of people… Yet history is made by the masses.'

Knowing how and when to advance what forms of

propaganda and agitation requires real experience. Listening to what workers are saying, understanding what they think is possible, judging what they are willing to do – all this bears upon what kinds of propaganda and what agitational demands should be advanced at any time.

There is a sect on the British left that has advanced the slogan 'General Strike Now!' in response to every industrial dispute of any size for many decades. On nearly all occasions, this had no resonance among even the advanced layers of workers. It is not that it would not be a good idea in the abstract (like socialist revolution itself). But the slogan hardly ever had any capacity to generate action.

Yet at certain points during the miners' strike of 1984-85, when the level of class-wide anger was massive and the desire to aid the miners very strong, the call for the union leaders to organise a general strike did have a purchase on the minds of many activists.

What this points to is that the judgement about forms of propaganda and agitation depends on a prior assessment of the condition of working class struggle. What is the balance of forces between workers, employers, and government? Which issues are in the forefront of workers' minds? What are the key arguments in the movement? These are all questions that need to be addressed when discussing the focus of party propaganda and agitation.

As Lenin said about *both* agitation and propaganda: 'propaganda and agitation alone are not enough for an entire class, the broad masses of the working people, those oppressed by capital, to take up such a stand. For that, the masses must have their own political experience…'

It is only by going through these experiences as part of the working class, learning from this experience in interaction with the working class, that revolutionaries can formulate appropriate propaganda and agitation.

Moreover, they have to adapt their ideological and political stance constantly according to how these ideas are received and acted upon in the struggle.

10. The united front

A network of the revolutionary minority must, as we have discussed in previous chapters, find ways of uniting with wider sections of the working class. Many of these workers will be organised in political parties that are, in general political terms, the opponents of revolutionaries, most obviously Labour Party-type, social-democratic parties.

The necessity for this kind of unity is obvious: workers are strongest when they are united, and there are all sorts of battles that have to be fought long before a revolutionary situation in which a majority of workers agree with the revolutionaries.

If revolutionary and Labour Party-supporting workers were to allow their political differences to divide them over trade union struggles, or anti-war campaigns, or in the fight against fascism, the ruling class would find it easier to defeat us. Leon Trotsky confronted this issue most sharply in the 1930s, when he was advising revolutionaries in Germany on how to respond to the growing threat of Hitler's Nazis.

The German Communist Party (CP), under the direction of Stalin, refused to unite with the Social Democratic Party (SPD). The Social Democrats, argued the CP, were supporters of capitalism, and capitalism bred fascism. How can we beat the fascists, they asked, if we do not take on capitalism? And the Social Democrats support capitalism, so we cannot unite with them. They even went so far as to describe the Social Democrats as 'social fascists'. In response, Trotsky told one of Aesop's fables:

A cattle dealer once drove some bulls to the slaughter-house. And the butcher came nigh with his sharp knife.

"Let's close ranks and jack up this executioner on our horns," suggested one of the bulls.

"If you please, in what way is the butcher any worse than the dealer who drove us hither with his cudgel?" replied the bulls, who had received their political education in Manuilsky's [Stalinist] institute.

"But we shall be able to attend to the dealer afterwards!"

"Nothing doing," replied the bulls, firm in their principles, to the counsellor. *"You are trying to shield our enemies from the left; you are a social-butcher yourself."*

And they refused to close ranks.

This, tragically, was the story of a death foretold. Even though the combined vote, to say nothing of the organised political weight, of the CP and SPD was greater than that of the Nazis when Hitler came to power, the failure to unite led to the destruction of the German working class movement, the Second World War, and the Holocaust.

In urging a united front, Trotsky was drawing on his experience in the Russian Revolution. Here, unity was achieved and a successful revolution resulted. The crucial episode came in the summer of 1917.

The weakness of the Provisional Government that had taken power in the February Revolution had disappointed its working class and peasant supporters and emboldened its Tsarist enemies. In the summer of 1917, the Government, under the leadership of moderate socialist Alexander Kerensky, faced an attempted right-wing military coup led by the Tsarist general Kornilov.

That summer, Kerensky had been cracking down on the revolutionary left – Trotsky was jailed, Lenin forced into hiding. It was this that had emboldened the Kornilov plotters. Indeed, until the last moment, Kerensky was directly encouraging the coup. Many Bolsheviks were, understandably, reluctant to defend the Kerensky government. But Lenin and Trotsky insisted that the Kornilov coup was the greater and more immediate danger, and that the Bolsheviks must unite with supporters of the Provisional Government to defeat the coup.

Trotsky later went so far as to say that if Kornilov had succeeded, the word for fascism would have been a Russian term. But the Bolsheviks did unite with the supporters of the Provisional Government. Through the workers' councils, they organised the defence of the revolution, crucially by arming the workers, and Kornilov was defeated.

This success shifted the balance of forces in two ways. Firstly, it shifted power from the enfeebled Provisional Government to the workers' councils. Secondly, it shifted political influence in the direction of the revolutionaries and away from moderate socialists like Kerensky.

As Lenin had said in the heat of battle:

Even now we must not support the Kerensky government. This is unprincipled. We may be asked: aren't we going to fight against Kornilov? Of course we must! … We shall fight, we are fighting against Kornilov, just as Kerensky's troops do, but we do not support Kerensky. On the contrary, we expose his weakness.

The successful defensive united front against Kornilov paved the way for the October Revolution. But this was only possible because the Bolsheviks retained their own specific, independent political organisation within the united front.

The united front was a limited political agreement for common action, not a programme for general political unity or the dissolution of the Bolshevik Party into a broad working class coalition.

The Bolsheviks kept up their criticism of the Kerensky government even while they were uniting with it to defeat Kornilov. Had they not done so, Kerensky would have emerged from the defeat of Kornilov to renew his persecution of the Bolsheviks. Once the decisive action was achieved, the Bolsheviks did not shy away from returning to their own independent political programme.

A powerful counter-example is provided by the example of the 'popular fronts' of the 1930s. Intially, when Trotsky urged a united front of all working class organisations to combat fascism, the Stalinist communist parties (CPs) took an ultra-left turn, rejecting any unity with the mainstream of the labour movement, which they derided as 'social fascists'.

But as the full calamity caused by this sectarian and divisive policy became apparent, the CPs turned 180° and adopted the policy of the popular front.

Trotsky's united front was a call for the unity of working class parties, crucially the Communist Party and the Social Democratic Party in Germany. It therefore aimed to unite all those workers who had a class interest in opposing fascism, even if they might disagree on how to achieve socialism.

The popular front, by contrast, wanted to unite working class organisations with middle class, liberal, and bourgeois parties – it was a 'people's' front, not a workers' front. The danger was clear: sections of the middle class may have had a temporary reason to oppose fascism, but, unlike workers, their whole existence as a class was not under threat. This made middle-class opposition to fascism lukewarm and vacillating.

And the cost was very high. The popular front limited the actions of the working class by subordinating them to their bourgeois allies – who might be frightened off by radicalism and militancy in the struggle.

Any mass united front may well attract individuals and currents from within the middle class – but the policy, action, and direction cannot be set by, or subordinated to, these elements. It is a question of who is leading whom. In the united front, the working class parties set the direction;

in the popular front, the working class parties are reduced to tailing a policy set by bourgeois parties.

The lessons are these. Revolutionaries should seek unity in action with the widest possible working class forces. They should oppose formal alliances with bourgeois organisations that will limit the action of the working class. And they should always maintain their own independence, seeking to influence and win other workers at the same time as uniting against common enemies.

This can be done only by building working class unity in struggle and revolutionary organisation at the same time.

11. Ultra-leftism

Lenin observed that for a vanguard party to perform its function properly, it must always be in touch with the rearguard. It must encourage and organise action by the majority of the class, or at least by the widest possible layers of the class beyond its own ranks. It cannot substitute the actions of its own members for those of the workers.

'Ultra-leftism' is the term given to those slogans and actions that attempt to substitute the actions of the militant minority for that of the majority of workers. The most graphic example of this policy is the behaviour of the German Communist Party in March 1921.

Germany was in a highly-charged political crisis after the revolution of 1918 that overthrew the Kaiser and ended Germany's participation in the First World War.

Huge class battles swept the country, at one time providing opportunities for revolution, at others opening the door to armed counter-revolution.

In 1921, a combination of intervention from the newly-formed Communist International in Moscow and home-grown ultra-lefts in Germany itself forced through a new tactical turn in the German Communist Party. The existing line of the Communist Party was criticised as too passive and in need of 'activising'. Karl Radek and Bela Kun, the representatives of the Communist International, urged the party to 'go on to the offensive' in order to shock workers out of their passivity, 'if necessary by a provocation', and force them to confront the government.

When the social-democratic President of Prussian Saxony announced a police crackdown on industrial areas, this policy of 'forcing the revolution' was activated.

The party paper ran an editorial on 20 March headed 'Who is not with me is against me: a word to social-democratic and independent workers'. It was an ultimatum to workers, telling them they must choose sides in the coming struggles.

The party called for and organised a general strike (the day before the factories were due to close for the Easter holidays), with the occupation of factories and the arming of workers. But the mood in the working class was not revolutionary, and the tactic was a disaster, pitting Communist Party workers against the non-Communist Party majority.

In Berlin, the strike was practically non-existent. Elsewhere, armed Communists clashed with workers as they went into the factories. In Hamburg, in an exchange of gunfire, dock workers drove off CP-supporting dockers and unemployed workers who had occupied the quays.

Estimates of the number who heeded the strike call vary between 200,000 and 500,000 – in a country with a working class of many millions, and where the Communist Party itself claimed no less than 500,000 members. It had ended, as one Central Committee member had predicted it would, with the 50 or so CP members who formed the core of the party in each workplace ranged against fellow workers who would, and often had, followed their lead in other circumstances.

The adventurism of the 'March Action' isolated the vanguard of the class and put reaction in the ascendant. The lesson of Lenin's *Left-wing communism: an infantile disorder*, written a year earlier, now stood out in the sharpest possible relief:

> *While the first historical objective (that of winning over the class conscious vanguard of the proletariat to the side of soviet power and the dictatorship of the working class) could not have been reached without a complete ideological and political victory over opportunism and social chauvinism, the second and immediate objective, which consists in being able to lead the masses to a new position ensuring the victory*

of the vanguard in the revolution, cannot be reached
without the liquidation of Left doctrinarism.

In this battle, Lenin argues, 'propagandist methods
alone, the mere repetition of the truths of "pure"
communism, are of no avail'. What is necessary is that the
slogans and actions of the revolutionaries point out the
next, most pressing, step in the struggle, not simply the
ultimate goal of the struggle.

But to know what the next step is, revolutionaries
must be in close contact with the mass of workers and
must judge both what the most urgent problem is and
what the next possible step might be. Only then can a
vanguard organisation unite with the majority of the
class in taking that step. If the revolutionaries attempt to
'leap over' the current consciousness of the class, they will
divide themselves from even the best non-party workers,
damaging their own organisation, the wider working-class
movement, and the relationship between the two.

12. Marxism and the trade unions

Trade unions are the basic defence mechanism of the working class. They were first built to defend workers at the point of production from employers' attacks on wages and conditions. They work best when they organise the widest possible sections of the working class irrespective of political, religious, ethnic, or any other kind of distinction. The old trade union slogans are, in this sense, fundamental truths: unity is strength; united we stand, divided we fall.

For these reasons, the first and fundamental job of any socialist at work is to build and strengthen trade union organisation wherever possible. But that is just the start of the problem.

Precisely because trade unions organise over the most basic economic questions, and because they aim to organise all workers – from the most politically conscious to the most conservative – a question arises about the relationship between the politically conscious minority and the rest of the unionised workforce.

If we return to Trotsky's metaphor of five workers with different outlooks (that is, uneven consciousness), then, in this case, we might imagine that all five workers are in the union together. Moreover, since trade unions exist within capitalism in order to bargain over the conditions under which labour is exploited – and not to abolish capitalism and exploitation – they inevitably exist in a state of compromise with the system. Even the most militant and successful strike will end with significant improvements for workers within *a still-existing capitalist system*. And many strikes will end with compromises that are worse than this.

There is, therefore, a contradictory pressure within the unions. On the one hand, there is the constant spur to organisation and action provided by employers' attempts to worsen conditions, lengthen hours, intensify work, and lower wages. On the other, the necessary class-wide organisation of the unions introduces an element of conservatism, and, because compromise is inevitable at some point in every union struggle, the more conservative members are encouraged to push for compromise sooner rather than later, settling for less rather than more.

Moreover, the longer unions exist and the more stable they become, the more likely they are to develop a conservative layer of full-time officials. These officials, especially those higher up the union structure, no longer feel the daily pressure of those still at work. They are likely to enjoy better conditions and higher pay than those they represent. They meet with employers and government ministers far more often than any ordinary trade unionist is ever likely to do.

In many instances, union officials will also be members of the Labour Party. This reinforces their conservative tendencies, because the Labour Party's official doctrine is to seek reform, and therefore compromise, within the capitalist system. When the Labour Party is in government, the pressure to compromise is even greater.

Under these circumstances, there exists an intense pressure for trade union officials to cease representing the interests of their members to employers and government, and instead to represent the interests of employers and government to their members.

To counter this pressure, rank-and-file organisation is desirable whenever it can be built. Rank-and-file organisations bring together ordinary workers and their most immediate elected representatives (shop stewards and office representatives) in union-wide or sectional organisation that can act as a counter-weight to the conservative pressure of full-time officials and give a lead to the rest of the workforce.

Such rank-and-file organisation, through meetings and bulletins, seeks to maximise the militant impulse of workers to defend themselves and to minimise the influence of officials who wish to dampen down the struggle.

But it is also necessary for a revolutionary organisation to maintain its own profile, both within the unions and in any rank-and-file organisations that it can assist in building. The organisational and political independence of the advanced minority is extremely important in the trade unions precisely because it is here that the direct mechanisms for transmitting the views of the employers and the government, and the pressure of the more conservative workers, can be most effective in disrupting the action of the working class.

There are many important lessons to be learned from the great General Strike of 1926. One of them, highlighted by Trotsky, is the way in which the pressure of the ruling class is transmitted into the working class movement.

Trotsky's point was that the government did not simply defeat the strike 'militarily' so to say. Nor did it exercise only direct ideological pressure on the working class movement. Rather, pressure was exercised indirectly through the intermediary layers of the Labour movement, especially its leaders. But the ultimate success even of this form of pressure depended on the political weakness of the left at the end of the chain of influence.

Trotsky saw that the government put pressure on the Labour Party leaders, the Labour Party leaders put pressure on the TUC, the right-wing of the TUC put pressure on the left-wing, and they in turn put pressure on the Minority Movement, the Communist Party-initiated rank-and-file movement of shop stewards. And finally, the Minority Movement, those who stood closest to the Communist Party, pressurised the Communist Party itself – whose resistance to the sell-out collapsed.

The Minority Movement, embracing almost a million workers, seemed very promising, but it bore the germs of destruction within itself. The masses knew as leaders of the movement only [trade union leaders] Purcell, Hicks, and Cook, whom, moreover, Moscow vouched for. These "left" friends, in a serious test, shamefully betrayed the proletariat. The revolutionary workers were thrown into confusion, sank into apathy, and naturally extended their disappointment to the Communist Party itself, which had only been the passive part of this whole mechanism of betrayal and perfidy. The Minority Movement was reduced to zero; the Communist Party returned to the existence of a negligible sect. In this way, thanks to a radically false conception of the party, the greatest movement of the English proletariat, which led to the General Strike, not only did not shake the apparatus of the reactionary bureaucracy, but, on the contrary, reinforced it, and compromised Communism in Britain for a long time.

In this case, as Trotsky explains, a critical weakness was introduced into the Communist Party's politics by pressure from the Stalinist bureaucracy in Moscow. Stalin wanted foreign allies and he soft-pedalled criticism of the British trade union leaders in the hope they would assist this project.

But the warning stands without the peculiarity of Stalin's influence. The state will always try to exercise influence through the union bureaucracy. And the reformist politics of the union bureaucracy will always lead them to try and transmit this pressure to the rank-and-file, using left-wing allies who are not sufficiently strong to resist them.

This underlines the importance of the political and organisational independence of the revolutionary minority. If – and this moment should be avoided if it can be – there comes a moment when the allies of yesterday become the channel for compromise today, the party must assert its independence even from its closest friends.

Long before the General Strike, in 1915, the rank-and-file organisation, the Clyde Workers Committee, had summed up the right attitude towards the trade union leaders:

> *We will support the officials just so long as they rightly represent the workers, but we will act independently immediately they misrepresent them.*

Trotsky was only paraphrasing the same sentiment when he wrote:

> *With the masses – always; with the vacillating leaders – sometimes, but only so long as they stand at the head of the masses. It is necessary to make use of the vacillating leaders while the masses are pushing them ahead, without for a minute abandoning criticism of these leaders.*

13. The Marxist method

There is prejudice about intellectual thought in our society, boosted by academia, which assumes that the greatest heights of theoretical achievement are the furthest from practical politics. Whether these are philosophical questions about the nature of human experience and the fundamentals of ethical choice or natural-scientific questions about the origin of the universe and the structure of the atom, they all seem a long way from our everyday issue of what to do next.

But for Marxists, the very opposite is true. The question 'what is to be done?' is very closely linked with issues about the Marxist method of analysis – in other words, with questions of Marxist philosophy.

Why is this? Can we not simply get by with the kind of ideas about strategy and tactics that have already been discussed in this pamphlet – the united front, sectarianism, ultra-leftism, and so on? Obviously, these concepts are essential, but how do we know when it is the right time to deploy a particular tactic? The Bolsheviks, as we have seen, almost missed the right time for the revolution in October 1917. But, as we have also seen, the German Communist Party's call for revolution in March 1921 was a catastrophe.

The bad news is that there is no guarantee. The good news is that there are two kinds of experience that can give an organisation the best chance of making these judgements correctly.

The first kind of experience is the struggle itself. A network that has many members rooted in the battles of the working class will have had to make these kinds of judgements, or less dramatic versions of the same kinds of judgements, over and over again. Its members will have learnt how to evaluate the moods of its own class, the character of the labour movement leaders, the nature of the police and media, and so on.

Roots in the class should inform the party about the most pressing questions for workers and what action is already being taken, and this can form the basis of judgements about how to respond. But this kind of experience is never enough on its own.

No situation is ever an exact repeat of the past; it always contains something new. And no situation ever interprets itself; it always requires an act of intellectual labour to explain it. Despite the old aphorism, the facts never speak for themselves. They always require interpretation. As Marx said, 'if appearance and reality coincided, there would be no need for science'.

So a second kind of experience is necessary: theoretical experience. This kind of experience gives us a method by which we can interpret the struggle. The starting point of any such analysis is to grasp the contradictory nature of our society. We have seen at the start of the pamphlet how the need for a vanguard organisation arises from the existence of contradictory consciousness among workers. And we have also seen that this contradictory consciousness arises from the interaction of oppression and revolt that is in the nature of wage-labour under capitalism. This in turn rests on the fundamental contradiction of capitalist society – that it requires the collective labour of workers to produce wealth, but that capitalists privately appropriate that wealth when it is produced.

We see here, in simplified sketch form, a series of interlinked contradictions, each resting on the other, which run from the fundamental economic structure of capitalism, through the consciousness of workers, to the forms of organisation most effective in acting on these contradictions. But this series of contradictions only describes the most general, and therefore relatively timeless, aspects of the system.

To analyse a new strategic and tactical situation would need much closer and more careful analysis. But the approach would be the same: first analyse the most general objective economic, social, and political contradictions. Then examine the contradictory forms of consciousness and organisations that arise from these. Then carefully specify what forms of organisation, slogans, demands, and so on might be expected to act on these contradictions in such ways as to advance the struggle. Finally, develop the organisational tools capable of realising these tactics.

Lenin was insistent that only a 'concrete analysis of a concrete situation' could be a guide to action. In criticism of an analysis of the possibilities of revolution in China by one of his fellow Bolshevik leaders, Nicholas Bukharin, Lenin wrote:

> I know next to nothing about the insurgents and revolutionaries of South China [but]…since there are uprisings, it is not too far-fetched to assume a controversy between Chinese No 1, who says that insurrection is a product of a most acute nation-wide class struggle, and Chinese No 2, who says that insurrection is an art. That is all I need to know to write a thesis à la Bukharin: "On the one hand…on the other hand." The one has failed to reckon with the art "factor", and the other with the "acuteness factor", etc. Because no concrete study has been made of this particular controversy, question, approach, etc., the result is dead, empty eclecticism.

Lenin insisted that 'the truth is always concrete'. In each case, generalities may or may not apply and will certainly occur and combine in unique ways. This is why a concrete analysis is always necessary.

At the point where revolutionaries took the step of initiating the Stop the War Coalition in 2001, we undertook an analysis something like this. We had already understood the nature of the new imperialism from theoretical work at the end of the Cold War, during the First Gulf War, and during the war in the Balkans. We understood the contradiction between expansive US military power and its relative economic decline. We judged, from preceding experience in the anti-globalisation movement, that there would be a mood to resist and that the left might not be divided in the way it had been in the Cold War.

The judgement, the analysis of the contradictions and the assessment of the consciousness of the class, might have been wrong, but the immediate reports of activists in the workplaces in the days after the attack on the World Trade Centre suggested they were not. The success of the first Stop the War rally in London, only 10 days after 9/11, proved it. Had it not, practice would have dictated a rethink of theory!

Crucial to this method, and what makes it essentially different from the normal method of science, is that it includes within it the subjective element. And this is not simply in the exterior sense that it requires a judgement about workers' consciousness, but in the additional sense that it must calculate the effect of our actions as organised revolutionaries on the objective situation. It must try to tell us not simply what is, but also what might be if we act on the objective situation in certain ways.

As Lenin argued:

> The objectivist speaks of the necessity of a given historical process, the materialist gives an exact picture of a given socio-economic formation and the antagonistic relations to which it gives rise. When demonstrating the necessity of a given series of facts, the objectivist always runs the risk of becoming an apologist for the facts; the materialist discloses the class contradictions and so defines his standpoint… the materialist would not content himself with stating insurmountable "historical tendencies", but

would point to the existence of certain classes which determine the content of a given system and preclude the possibility of any solution except by the action of the producers themselves...materialism includes partisanship, so to speak, and enjoins the direct and open adoption of the standpoint of a definite social group in the assessment of events.

In summarising Lenin's application of the Marxist method in this field, Georg Lukacs wrote:

He studied in order to learn how to apply the dialectic; to learn how to discover, by concrete analyses of concrete situations, the specific in the general and the general in the specific; to see in the novelty of a situation what connects it with former developments; to observe the perpetually new phenomena constantly produced under the laws of historical development; to detect the part in the whole and the whole in the part; to find in historical necessity the moment of activity and in activity the connection with historical necessity.

And Lukacs concluded:

Leninism represents a hitherto unprecedented degree of concrete, unschematic, unmechanistic, purely praxis-oriented thought. To preserve this is the task of the Leninist.

Further reading

If you have found this short introduction interesting
you might also like to read the following:

Karl Marx and Frederick Engels,
The Communist Manifesto

V I Lenin,
What is to be Done?
Left-wing communism: an infantile disorder

Leon Trotsky,
Lessons of October
The Struggle Against Fascism in Germany

Georg Lukacs
Lenin: a study in the unity of his thought

Tony Cliff
Lenin
4 volumes, but especially V*olume 1: Building the Party*